Wingo the Superhero

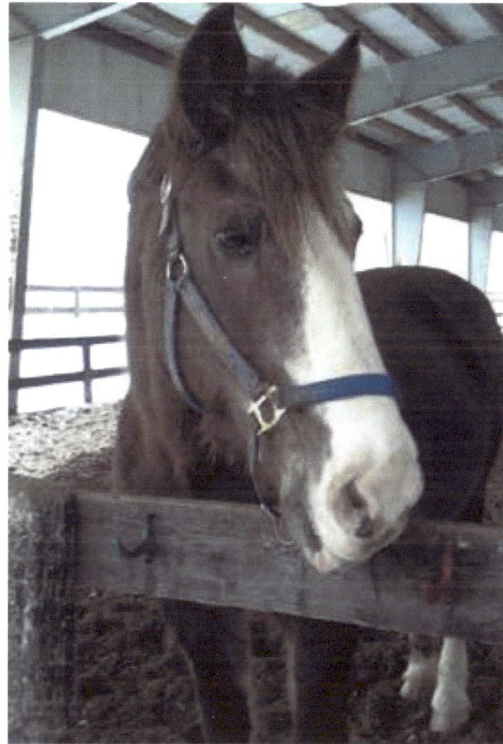

BARBARA MILLER

STUDIO OF BOOKS
THE SPACE FOR YOUR MESSAGE

Studio of Books LLC
5900 Balcones Drive Suite 100
Austin, Texas 78731
www.studioofbooks.org
Hotline: (254) 800-1183

Ordering Information:
Special discounts are available on quantity purchases by corporations, associations, and others. For details, contact the publisher at the address above.

Printed in the United States of America.

ISBN-13:   Softcover   978-1-968491-48-2
           eBook   978-1-968491-49-9

Library of Congress Control Number: 2025916858

In memory of Kevin Gowl

Friends come in many colors, shapes, and sizes. One of my best friends is Wingo, my beautiful horse. He is my hero, and this story is just one reason why I feel this way.

One frigid Friday evening in March, it was beginning to snow on the farm where Wingo the horse lived. Word around the barn was that this storm was going to be the biggest storm ever in the area. There were already four inches of snow on the ground! The stable hands had seen many snow storms, but they knew this one was going to be a challenge. Horses in the fields would have to get food and water to weather the intensity of the coming storm. Kevin, the barn manager, was getting worried because the weather forecast reported that there could be two feet of new snow by Saturday evening.

Wingo, my strong huge horse, was standing in his stall listening to the hustle and bustle of the stable hands getting feed and water buckets ready. Wingo had heard about the possible two more feet of snow, and he was also getting worried about the horses that lived in the fields.

Wingo said to the other horses, "We need to help Kevin and the stable hands to keep all our friends safe from this storm." Sandy and Willie, Wingo's best friends, agreed with Wingo and said they would do anything to help. Wingo decided to talk to the horses in the other barns. He was sure they would help out too.

Wingo left his barn and made his rounds to check with horses in the other two barns. The other horses had also heard Kevin talking to the stable hands and were getting nervous about their friends out in the field. Wingo reassured them that it would be okay.

Dazzle asked Wingo, "How are we going to help? We can't carry hay and grain out to the fields. We're not strong enough!"

Wingo agreed that the other horses were not strong enough to carry the large amounts of hay and grain that would be needed. He pondered this while walking back to his stall. Outside, the snow was starting to get very heavy, and the wind was starting to gust. The weather conditions made it miserable for anyone or anything to be out in the field.

That night, the barn doors had been closed against the awful weather. Wingo and his barn mates started to talk about the storm and how the horses in the field would survive. Willie said, "Hopefully the storm won't be as bad as they say it's going to be!"

That night, Wingo couldn't sleep at all. The wind howled so loudly, and the window of Wingo's stall was covered with snow. Then it came to him. He would share his plan with Kevin and the other horses the next day.

The next morning, the snow was so high that it was difficult for Kevin to make his way to the barn where Wingo and his friends were stabled.

Kevin came to Wingo's stall and said, "We had easily one foot of snow overnight, and it's still coming down! I don't know how we are going to get to the other horses in the field."

Wingo said, "Don't worry. I have an idea! I'm big and strong, and I can carry the hay and feed to the horses in the field."

Kevin agreed that this was a great idea. He made sure to bundle up, then harnessed Wingo to a sled large enough to carry hay, grain, and water. He jumped onto Wingo's back. Wingo bravely plowed through the snow and howling wind and made it to the first field. Kevin jumped off of Wingo and fed the horses that were waiting for their breakfast. He and Wingo also visited the water trough and added warm water to it. Kevin smiled and patted Wingo proudly as he realized the plan was working!

One by one, Kevin and Wingo made their way around to all of the fields. By the end of the morning, all of the outside horses had had breakfast, big fluffy piles of hay, and warm water in their troughs.

That night, Kevin and Wingo were able to sleep soundly knowing that all the horses were safe and cared for. On Saturday morning, the snow finally stopped, and the sun broke through. The path that Kevin and Wingo had made through the snow was still clear enough that they could use it to go around and feed the outside horses over the next couple of days.

Thanks to Wingo and his bravery and good thinking, the farm felt peaceful and safe again. All the horses in the fields called him their hero. Kevin named him Wingo the Superhero!

This story, along with many others, is one reason why he's my hero and my friend too!

About the Author

Barbara Miller was in love with horses from a very early age. Her uncle Willie would take her to the racetrack every day, and while he was looking to place his bet, she was looking at the majesty of each horse—the hugeness but also the gracefulness while running each race. He would take her to the paddock, and there she was able to get a closer look at these incredible animals. Since then Barbara has lived and ridden and cared for these amazing creatures.

www.ingramcontent.com/pod-product-compliance
Lightning Source LLC
Chambersburg PA
CBHW041551030426

42335CB00004B/186